Country Music

TRIVIA

500 QUESTIONS

IDENTIFY THE ARTIST

Jim McLain

The author is not responsible for any mistakes in the name of the song or the artist. Every attempt has been made to identify the current or original artist, knowing that many of the songs have been performed by other artists.

This first book of Trivia is dedicated to my late wife and daughter, (Mary McLain and Erin McLain, M.D., F.A.A.P.) Their love and support of my love of trivia lead me to writing this book.

Printed in the United States of America

First Printing August 2019

ISBN 978-1-64633-042-3 Paperback

Published by:

Book Services
www.BookServices.us

1. Sink the Bismarck
   a. Johnny Cash
   b. Johnny Horton
   c. Trace Adkins
   d. Randy Travis

2. Okie from Muskogee
   a. Willie Nelson
   b. Garth Brooks
   c. Neal McCoy
   d. Merle Haggard

3. Ring of Fire
   a. Kenny Rogers
   b. Johnny Cash
   c. Merle Haggard
   d. Willie Nelson

4. Folsom Prison Blues
   a. Alan Jackson
   b. Vince Gill
   c. Kenny Rogers
   d. Johnny Cash

5. Fool No. 1
   a. Tammy Wynette
   b. Loretta Lynn
   c. Brenda Lee
   d. Tina Turner

6. Yesterday, When I Was Young
   a. John Anderson
   b. Roy Clark
   c. Rhett Adkins
   d. Conway Twitty

7. Are You Lonesome Tonight?
   a. Elvis Presley
   b. Garth Brooks
   c. Brooks & Dunn
   d. Tim McGraw

8. Six Days on the Road
   a. Toby Keith
   b. Willie Nelson
   c. Clint Black
   d. Dave Dudley

9. Jackson
   a. Johnny Cash & June Carter Cash
   b. The Oak Ridge Boys
   c. Alabama
   d. Granger Smith

10. Wonder Could I Live There Anymore
    a. Glen Campbell
    b. Kenny Rogers
    c. Charley Pride
    d. Billy Dean

11. Bad Boy
    a. Tim McGraw
    b. Conway Twitty
    c. Dwight Yoakam
    d. Chris Stapleton

12. Beggar to a King
    a. Joe Diffie
    b. Vince Gill
    c. Hank Snow
    d. Trace Adkins

13. What's Made Milwaukee Famous
    (Has Made a Loser Out of Me)
    a. John Conlee
    b. Don Williams
    c. Jerry Lee Lewis
    d. Michael Ray

14. Saginaw, Michigan
    a. Lefty Frizzell
    b. George Ducas
    c. Dustin Lynch
    d. Clay Walker

15. The Window Up Above
    a. Ray Price
    b. Clint Black
    c. Aaron Tippin
    d. George Jones

16. Have You Ever Been Lonely
    a. Tim McGraw & Faith Hill
    b. Jim Reeves & Patsy Cline
    c. Johnny Cash & June Cash
    d. Garth Brooks & Trisha Yearwood

17. She's Got You
    a. Patsy Cline
    b. Dolly Parton
    c. Patty Loveless
    d. Nina Simone

18. Almost Persuaded
    a. Old Dominion
    b. David Houston
    c. Sam Hunt
    d. Kane Brown

19. Can't Help Falling in Love
    a. Jerry Reed
    b. Guy Clark
    c. Kix Brooks
    d. Elvis Presley

20. Dang Me
    a. Josh Turner
    b. Roger Miller
    c. Alan Jackson
    d. Rhett Adkins

21. Big Bad John
    a. Kenny Rogers
    b. John Denver
    c. Jimmy Dean
    d. Billy Dean

22. Girl on the Billboard
    a. Del Reeves
    b. Cole Swindell
    c. Kenny Chesney
    d. Randy Travis

23. Darling, You Know I Wouldn't Lie
    a. Conway Twitty
    b. Neal McCoy
    c. Kris Kristofferson
    d. Jamey Johnson

24. I'm Sorry
    a. Wynonna Judd
    b. Brenda Lee
    c. Tanya Tucker
    d. Tammy Wynette

25. Excuse Me (I Think I've Got
    a Heartache)
    a. Rascal Flatts
    b. Clay Walker
    c. Collin Raye
    d. Buck Owens

26. Georgia on My Mind
    a. Ray Charles
    b. Ryan Bingham
    c. Craig Morgan
    d. Lyle Lovett

27. Green, Green Grass Of Home
    a. Porter Wagoner
    b. Waylon Jennings
    c. Roy Clark
    d. Toby Keith

28. Just One Time
    a. Dave Dudley
    b. Don Gibson
    c. Charley Pride
    d. George Jones

29. South of The Border (Down Mexico Way)
    a. Patsy Cline
    b. Kate Bush
    c. Deana Carter
    d. Pam Tillis

30. Ode to Billy Joe
    a. Trisha Yearwood
    b. Bobbie Gentry
    c. Dolly Parton
    d. Grace Jones

31. Ruby, Don't Take Your Love to Town
    a. Brothers Osborne
    b. Alabama
    c. The Oak Ridge Boys
    d. Kenny Rogers & The First Edition

32. Let Your Love Flow
    a. The Bellamy Brothers
    b. Brooks & Dunn
    c. Josh Turner
    d. Ed Bruce

33. I Overlooked an Orchid
    a. Mickey Gilley
    b. Trace Adkins
    c. Conway Twitty
    d. Elvis Presley

34. Don't It Make My Brown Eyes Blue
    a. Tammy Wynette
    b. Loretta Lynn
    c. Faith Hill
    d. Crystal Gayle

35. The Gambler
    a. Tim McGraw
    b. Kenny Rogers
    c. The Oak Ridge Boys
    d. Waylon Jennings

36. I Was Country, When Country Wasn't Cool
    a. Barbara Mandrell & George Jones
    b. Reba McEntire
    c. Jo Dee Messina
    d. Shania Twain

37. Coal Miner's Daughter
    a. Wynonna Judd
    b. Little Big Town
    c. Loretta Lynn
    d. LeAnn Rimes

38. Save The Last Dance for Me
    a. Kathy Mattea
    b. Emmylou Harris
    c. Lorrie Morgan
    d. Maren Morris

39. Listen To a Country Song
    a. Lynn Anderson
    b. Kelsea Ballerini
    c. Deana Carter
    d. Trisha Yearwood

40. Backside of Thirty
    a. Keith Whitney
    b. Jerry Reed
    c. John Conlee
    d. John Anderson

41. Amos Moses
    a. George Jones
    b. Jerry Reed
    c. Ronnie Milsap
    d. Clint Black

42. Lay Down Beside Me
    a. Don Williams
    b. Collin Raye
    c. Brett Young
    d. David Allan Coe

43. You've Never Been This Far Before
    a. Trace Adkins
    b. Clint Black
    c. Conway Twitty
    d. Marty Robbins

44. Country Sunshine
    a. Dixie Chicks
    b. Martina McBride
    c. Dottie West
    d. Carrie Underwood

45. Take This Job and Shove It
    a. Merle Haggard
    b. Jerry Reed
    c. Johnny Cash
    d. Johnny Paycheck

46. I Won't Mention It Again
    a. Ray Price
    b. Alan Jackson
    c. Tim McGraw
    d. Old Dominion

47. Bed of Roses
    a. Alabama
    b. The Oak Ridge Boys
    c. Statler Brothers
    d. Brothers Osborne

48. Rose Colored Glasses
    a. John Conlee
    b. John Anderson
    c. Joe Diffie
    d. Vince Gill

49. Soul Song
    a. Guy Clark
    b. Josh Turner
    c. Toby Keith
    d. Joe Stampley

50. It Was Almost Like a Song
    a. Ronnie Milsap
    b. Marty Robbins
    c. George Jones
    d. John Prine

51. Easy Livin'
    a. Tim McGraw
    b. Uriah Heep
    c. Josh Turner
    d. Guy Clark

52. You're the Best Thing That Ever
    Happened to Me
    a. Aaron Tippin
    b. Trace Adkins
    c. Ray Price
    d. Neal McCoy

53. (Old Dogs, Children and)
    Watermelon Wine
    a. Tom T. Hall
    b. Waylon Jennings
    c. Clay Walker
    d. Sawyer Brown

54. San Antonio Stroll
    a. Trisha Yearwood
    b. Tanya Tucker
    c. Jana Kramer
    d. Carrie Underwood

55. Funny Face
    a. Faith Hill
    b. Reba McEntire
    c. Jo Dee Messina
    d. Donna Fargo

56. Would You Lay With Me (In a Field Of Stone)
   a. Tanya Tucker
   b. Shania Twain
   c. Kathy Mattea
   d. Maren Morris

57. The Devil Went Down to Georgia
   a. Charlie Daniels Band
   b. Lonestar
   c. The Oak Ridge Boys
   d. Brothers Osborne

58. Daydreams About Night Things
   a. Ronnie Milsap
   b. Brooks & Dunn
   c. Ricky Van Shelton
   d. Keith Whitney

59. You Can't Be a Beacon (If Your Light Don't Shine)
   a. Martina McBride
   b. April Kry
   c. Donna Fargo
   d. Loretta Lynn

60. Before the Next Teardrop Falls
   a. Jerry Reed
   b. Rhett Adkins
   c. Freddy Fender
   d. Randy Travis

61. All the Gold in California
     a. Brothers Osborne
     b. The Oak Ridge Boys
     c. Kenny Rogers
     d. Larry Gatlin & The Gatlin
     Brothers Band

62. Stay Young
     a. Ray Price
     b. Big & Rich
     c. Don Williams
     d. Blake Shelton

63. (Ghost) Riders in The Sky
     a. The Bellamy Brothers
     b. Johnny Cash
     c. Kenny Rogers
     d. Sam Hunt

64. Rose Garden
     a. Lynn Anderson
     b. Loretta Lynn
     c. Trisha Yearwood
     d. Tina Turner

65. Two More Bottles of Wine
     a. Dixie Chicks
     b. Little Big Town
     c. Kelsea Ballerini
     d. Emmylou Harris

66. Sleeping Single in A Double Bed
    a. Barbara Mandrell
    b. Taylor Swift
    c. April Kry
    d. Carrie Underwood

67. One of These Days
    a. Deana Carter
    b. Emmylou Harris
    c. Faith Hill
    d. Lorrie Morgan

68. Blaze of Glory
    a. Jon Bon Jovi
    b. Tim McGraw
    c. Brooks & Dunn
    d. Rodney Atkins

69. 9 to 5
    a. Trisha Yearwood
    b. Patty Loveless
    c. Dolly Parton
    d. Pam Tillis

70. Cherokee Fiddle
    a. Johnny Lee
    b. John Cougar
    c. Joe Walsh
    d. Jason Aldean

71. American Made
    a. Creedence Clearwater Revival
    b. The Oak Ridge Boys
    c. Montgomery Gentry
    d. The Eagles

72. 72.Somebody's Knockin'
    a. Big & Rich
    b. Luke Bryan
    c. Terri Gibbs
    d. Justin Moore

73. America
    a. Garth Brooks
    b. Tim McGraw
    c. Waylon Jennings
    d. Blake Shelton

74. One Love at a Time
    a. Tanya Tucker
    b. Kelsea Ballerini
    c. Kacey Musgraves
    d. Faith Hill

75. Have Mercy
    a. Patty Loveless
    b. Nina Simone
    c. Tori Amos
    d. The Judds

76. You're the Reason God Made Oklahoma
    a. Florida Georgia Line
    b. David Frizzell & Shelly West
    c. Brooks & Dunn
    d. Alan Jackson

77. Much Too Young (To Feel This Damn Old)
    a. Dierks Bentley
    b. Garth Brooks
    c. Keith Urban
    d. Justin Moore

78. I Love a Rainy Night
    a. Eddie Rabbitt
    b. The Band Perry
    c. Jake Owen
    d. Lee Brice

79. The Ride
    a. Charlie Daniels Band
    b. Tractors
    c. David Allan Coe
    d. Emerson Drive

80. Why'd You Come in Here Lookin' Like That
    a. Loretta Lynn
    b. Shania Twain
    c. Carrie Underwood
    d. Dolly Parton

81. Amarillo by Morning
    a. Sam Hunt
    b. Dustin Lynch
    c. George Strait
    d. Keith Whitney

82. Big Ole Brew
    a. Mel McDaniel
    b. Tim McGraw
    c. George Ducas
    d. Neal McCoy

83. Dancin' Cowboys
    a. Emerson Drive
    b. The Tractors
    c. Brett Eldredge
    d. The Bellamy Brothers

84. Thirty-Nine and Holding
    a. Jerry Lee Lewis
    b. Randy Houser
    c. Bob Seger
    d. Eric Church

85. A Country Boy Can Survive
    a. Hank Williams, Jr.
    b. Joe Walsh
    c. Emerson Drive
    d. Dierks Bentley

86. Islands in The Stream
    a. Billy Currington
    b. The Tractors
    c. Kenny Rogers & Dolly Parton
    d. Keith Urban

87. Roll On (Eighteen Wheeler)
    a. Alabama
    b. The Band Perry
    c. Jake Owen
    d. Lee Brice

88. All My Rowdy Friends (Have Settled Down)
    a. Hank Williams, Jr.
    b. Big & Rich
    c. Luke Bryan
    d. Frankie Ballard

89. Am I Losing You?
    a. Canaan Smith
    b. Justin Moore
    c. Ronnie Milsap
    d. Brett Eldredge

90. Dixieland Delight
    a. Alabama
    b. Creedence Clearwater Revival
    c. John Cougar
    d. Joe Walsh

91. Feels So Right
    a. Alabama
    b. Jason Aldean
    c. Montgomery Gentry
    d. Florida Georgia Line

92. That's All That Matters to Me
    a. Eagles
    b. Mickey Gilley
    c. Keith Anderson
    d. Rodney Atkins

93. Baby I Lied
    a. Kacey Musgraves
    b. Deborah Allen
    c. Deana Carter
    d. Wynonna Judd

94. Queen of Hearts
    a. Juice Newton
    b. Tammy Wynette
    c. Maren Morris
    d. Kate Bush

95. She's My Rock
    a. Keith Whitney
    b. Tim McGraw
    c. Alan Jackson
    d. George Jones

96. You're the Best Break This Old Heart
    Ever Had
    a. Brooks & Dunn
    b. Alan Jackson
    c. Ed Bruce
    d. John Michael Montgomery

97. My Home's in Alabama
    a. Gary Allan
    b. Alabama
    c. Kenny Chesney
    d. Toby Keith

98. Highway 40 Blues
    a. Ricky Skaggs
    b. Clint Black
    c. Clay Walker
    d. Travis Tritt

99. I've Been Loved by the Best
    a. Brad Paisley
    b. Randy Travis
    c. Tracy Boyd
    d. Don Williams

100. Little Ways
    a. Ryan Bingham
    b. Dwight Yoakam
    c. Craig Morgan
    d. Josh Turner

101. God Bless the USA
    a. Guy Clark
    b. Jerry Reed
    c. Lee Greenwood
    d. Trace Adkins

102. Drivin' My Life Away
    a. Willie Nelson
    b. Waylon Jennings
    c. Kris Kristofferson
    d. Eddie Rabbitt

103. What's Forever For
    a. Michael Martin Murphey
    b. Florida Georgia Line
    c. John Michael Montgomery
    d. Ricky Van Shelton

104. He Got You
    a. Neal McCoy
    b. John Anderson
    c. Ronnie Milsap
    d. Billy Dean

105. Seven Year Ache
    a. Trisha Yearwood
    b. Rosanne Cash
    c. Kelsea Ballerini
    d. Carrie Underwood

106. Mountain of Love
     a. Collin Raye
     b. Charley Pride
     c. Sawyer Brown
     d. Bryan White

107. Turn It Loose
     a. Dwight Yoakam
     b. Clay Walker
     c. Vince Gill
     d. The Judds

108. He Stopped Loving Her Today
     a. Joe Diffie
     b. Alan Jackson
     c. Blake Shelton
     d. George Jones

109. Black Sheep
     a. John Anderson
     b. Brooks & Dunn
     c. Tim McGraw
     d. Rascal Flatts

110. The Church on Cumberland Road
     a. Johnny Cash
     b. Willie Nelson
     c. Kenny Rogers
     d. Shenandoah

111. Rest Your Love on Me
    a. Michael Ray
    b. Conway Twitty
    c. Old Dominion
    d. Dustin Lynch

112. Don't Close Your Eyes
    a. Chris Stapleton
    b. Sam Hunt
    c. Keith Whitley
    d. Thomas Rhett

113. If You're Thinking You Want
    a Stranger (There's One
    Coming Home)
    a. Cole Swindell
    b. Scott McCreey
    c. George Strait
    d. Kane Brown

114. Seven Spanish Angels
    a. Granger Smith
    b. Ray Charles & Willie Nelson
    c. Brothers Osborne
    d. The Oak Ridge Boys

115. There's No Way Getting Over Me
    a. Ronnie Milsap
    b. Ricky Van Shelton
    c. Keith Whitney
    d. Conway Twitty

116. Five Minutes
     a. Dixie Chicks
     b. Little Big Town
     c. Kate Bush
     d. Lorrie Morgan

117. I'll Always Come Back
     a. George Ducas
     b. K. T. Oslin
     c. Neal McCoy
     d. John Anderson

118. On The Road Again
     a. Brothers Osborne
     b. The Oak Ridge Boys
     c. Willie Nelson
     d. Trace Adkins

119. Independence Day
     a. Faith Hill
     b. Martina McBride
     c. Reba McEntire
     d. Deana Carter

120. That's as Close as I'll Get to
     Loving You
     a. John Anderson
     b. Rhett Adkins
     c. Trace Adkins
     d. Aaron Tippin

121. Born to Be Blue
    a. Taylor Swift
    b. Lorrie Morgan
    c. Tanya Tucker
    d. The Judds

122. Stand Beside Me
    a. Jo Dee Messina
    b. Faith Hill
    c. Grace Jones
    d. Kathy Mattea

123. God Blessed Texas
    a. Little Big Town
    b. Trace Adkins
    c. Little Texas
    d. Kenny Chesney

124. Passionate Kisses
    a. Reba McEntire
    b. Mary Chapin Carpenter
    c. Carrie Underwood
    d. Maren Morris

125. Down on The Farm
    a. Tim McGraw
    b. Joe Walsh
    c. Billy Currington
    d. Eric Church

126. Born Country
    a. The Oak Ridge Boys
    b. Brothers Osborne
    c. Alabama
    d. Brooks & Dunn

127. My Best Friend
    a. Tim McGraw
    b. Dierks Bentley
    c. Justin Moore
    d. Jake Owen

128. Stars Over Texas
    a. Luke Bryan
    b. Tracy Lawrence
    c. Ricochet
    d. Big & Rich

129. That's My Story
    a. John Cougar
    b. Collin Raye
    c. Jason Aldean
    d. Keith Anderson

130. Life's a Dance
    a. John Michael Montgomery
    b. Montgomery Gentry
    c. Josh Turner
    d. Chris Stapleton

131. Midnight in Montgomery
    a. Montgomery Gentry
    b. Aaron Tippin
    c. Alan Jackson
    d. John Michael Montgomery

132. Flat on The Floor
    a. Carrie Underwood
    b. Trisha Yearwood
    c. Dolly Parton
    d. Taylor Swift

133. In the Dream
    a. Craig Morgan
    b. The Eagles
    c. Keith Anderson
    d. Jason Aldean

134. Wish I Didn't Know Now
    a. Toby Keith
    b. Jamey Johnson
    c. Randy Travis
    d. Kenny Chesney

135. Baby Likes to Rock It
    a. Rascal Flatts
    b. Alan Jackson
    c. The Tractors
    d. Joe Diffie

136. What The Cowgirls Do
    a. Clay Walker
    b. Vince Gill
    c. Bryan White
    d. Sawyer Brown

137. My Maria
    a. Collin Raye
    b. Old Dominion
    c. Dustin Lynch
    d. Brooks & Dunn

138. Like the Rain
    a. Clint Black
    b. Chris Stapleton
    c. Sam Hunt
    d. Thomas Rhett

139. One Way Ticket (Because I Can)
    a. Maren Morris
    b. Taylor Swift
    c. April Kry
    d. LeAnn Rimes

140. Who's Cheatin' Who
    a. Cole Swindell
    b. Alan Jackson
    c. Kane Brown
    d. Granger Smith

141. Some Girls Do
    a. Ricky Van Shelton
    b. Sawyer Brown
    c. Keith Whitney
    d. George Ducas

142. Daddy's Come Around
    a. Neal McCoy
    b. John Anderson
    c. Paul Overstreet
    d. Rhett Adkins

143. I Like It, I Love It
    a. Tim McGraw
    b. Garth Brooks
    c. Trace Adkins
    d. Clint Black

144. That Don't Impress Me Much
    a. Kelsea Ballerini
    b. Taylor Swift
    c. Shania Twain
    d. Miranda Lambert

145. You'll Think of Me
    a. Brett Young
    b. Chris Janson
    c. Keith Urban
    d. Dylan Scott

146. Believe
   a. Brooks & Dunn
   b. Brett Young
   c. Luke Combs
   d. Chase Rice

147. I'm Gonna Love You Through It
   a. Lady Antebellum
   b. Ashley McBryde
   c. Maren Morris
   d. Martina McBride

148. Pontoon
   a. Little Big Town
   b. Dixie Chicks
   c. Taylor Swift
   d. Faith Hill

149. I'm Still a Guy
   a. Aaron Watson
   b. Aaron Tippin
   c. Brad Paisley
   d. Midland

150. Fast Cars and Freedom
   a. Rascal Flatts
   b. Kris Kristofferson
   c. Trace Adkins
   d. Josh Turner

151. Must Be Doin' Somethin' Right
    a. Chris Stapleton
    b. Billy Currington
    c. Keith Urban
    d. Jake Owen

152. You Look Good
    a. Carrie Underwood
    b. Lady Antebellum
    c. Miranda Lambert
    d. Taylor Swift

153. Mama Tried
    a. Brothers Osborne
    b. The Oak Ridge Boys
    c. Merle Haggard
    d. Alabama

154. The South's Gonna Do It Again
    a. The Charlie Daniels Band
    b. Willie Nelson
    c. Merle Haggard
    d. Brooks & Dunn

155. Woman to Woman
    a. Loretta Lynn
    b. Barbara Mandrell
    c. Tammy Wynette
    d. Patty Loveless

156. Forever and Ever, Amen
    a. Randy Travis
    b. Waylon Jennings
    c. Vince Gill
    d. Kenny Rogers

157. 15 Years Ago
    a. Conway Twitty
    b. Kenny Chesney
    c. Toby Keith
    d. Clint Black

158. My Woman, My Woman, My Wife
    a. Midland
    b. Aaron Watson
    c. Marty Robbins
    d. Chase Rice

159. Golden Ring
    a. George Jones & Tammy Wynette
    b. Tim McGraw & Faith Hill
    c. Garth Brooks & Trisha Yearwood
    d. The Bellamy Brothers

160. Heaven's Just a Sin Away
    a. Ray Price
    b. The Kendalls
    c. Big & Rich
    d. Blake Shelton

161. Daddy's Hands
    a. Donna Fargo
    b. Lynn Anderson
    c. Holly Dunn
    d. April Kry

162. Freedom to Stay
    a. Lonestar
    b. Waylon Jennings
    c. John Cougar
    d. Joe Walsh

163. Tulsa Time
    a. Kenny Rogers
    b. Tim McGraw
    c. Don Williams
    d. Brooks & Dunn

164. On My Knees
    a. Rodney Atkins
    b. The Eagles
    c. Big & Rich
    d. Jaci Velasquez

165. Older Women
    a. Luke Bryan
    b. Clint Black
    c. Ronnie McDowell
    d. Justin Moore

166. Easy Lovin'
     a. Freddie Hart
     b. Dierks Bentley
     c. Keith Urban
     d. Justin Moore

167. Take Your Time
     a. David Allan Coe
     b. Emerson Drive
     c. Sam Hunt
     d. Lee Brice

168. You Never Miss a Real Good Thing
     (Till He Says Goodbye)
     a. Faith Hill
     b. Crystal Gayle
     c. Kacey Musgraves
     d. Tanya Tucker

169. Blue Eyes Crying in the Rain
     a. Willie Nelson
     b. Sam Hunt
     c. Dustin Lynch
     d. Randy Travis

170. Here You Come Again
     a. Nina Simone
     b. Taylor Swift
     c. Little Big Town
     d. Dolly Parton

171. For the Good Times
    a. Jake Owen
    b. Neal McCoy
    c. Ray Price
    d. The Band Perry

172. Come Early Morning
    a. Eric Church
    b. Don Williams
    c. Bob Seger
    d. Randy Houser

173. Mr. Bojangles
    a. Big & Rich
    b. TheTractors
    c. The Oak Ridge Boys
    d. Nitty Gritty Dirt Band

174. If I said You Had A Beautiful Body,
    Would You Hold It Against Me?
    a. The Bellamy Brothers
    b. Dierks Bentley
    c. John Anderson
    d. Rhett Adkins

175. You Never Even Called Me by
    My Name
    a. Craig Morgan
    b. David Allan Coe
    c. Michael Martin Murphy
    d. Ronnie McDowell

176. Peter Pan
     a. Lee Ann Womack
     b. Brenda Lee
     c. Dixie Chicks
     d. Kelsea Ballerini

177. Speak to A Girl
     a. Tim McGraw & Faith Hill
     b. Dave Dudley
     c. Hank Snow
     d. John Conlee

178. Boy
     a. Don Williams
     b. Lee Brice
     c. Mickey Gilley
     d. Mel McDaniel

179. For the First Time
     a. Billy Currington
     b. Midland
     c. Darius Rucker
     d. Aaron Watson

180. You Broke Up With Me
     a. Walker Hayes
     b. Clint Black
     c. Randy Travis
     d. Trace Adkins

181. Take Back Home Girl
    a. Dylan Scott
    b. Chris Young
    c. Chase Rice
    d. Chris Lane & Tori Kelly

182. Get Out of This Town
    a. Miranda Lambert
    b. Lady Antebellum
    c. Carrie Underwood
    d. Ashley McBryde

183. Another Man's Woman
    a. Luke Combs
    b. Conway Twitty
    c. Justin Moore
    d. Chris Young

184. Drinkin' Problem
    a. Jake Owen
    b. Lee Brice
    c. Brett Eldredge
    d. Midland

185. Today
    a. Brad Paisley
    b. Josh Turner
    c. Guy Clark
    d. Craig Morgan

186. A Guy With a Girl
 a. Chris Stapleton
 b. Rhett Adkins
 c. Blake Shelton
 d. Neal McCoy

187. Fishin' in The Dark
 a. Toby Keith
 b. Gary Allan
 c. Nitty Gritty Dirt Band
 d. John Michael Montgomery

188. All the Pretty Girls
 a. Michael Ray
 b. Old Dominion
 c. Kenny Chesney
 d. Dustin Lynch

189. Sober Saturday Night
 a. Collin Raye
 b. Sawyer Brown
 c. Bryan White
 d. Chris Young & Vince Gill

190. Round Here Buzz
 a. Eric Church
 b. Clay Walker
 c. Vince Gill
 d. Joe Diffie

191. Light It Up
    a. Alan Jackson
    b. Luke Bryan
    c. Brooks & Dunn
    d. Kane Brown

192. Up Down
    a. Florida Georgia Line
    b. Keith Whitley
    c. Gary Allan
    d. Tracy Boyd

193. California
    a. Big & Rich
    b. Brooks & Dunn
    c. Kenny Chesney
    d. Toby Keith

194. Always on My MInd
    a. John Cougar
    b. Joe Walsh
    c. Willie Nelson
    d. Craig Morgan

195. Ask Me How I Know
    a. Florida Georgia Line
    b. Garth Brooks
    c. The Eagles
    d. Montgomery Gentry

196. Better Man
    a. Kathy Mattea
    b. Lorrie Morgan
    c. Tanya Tucker
    d. Little Big Town

197. Song for Another Time
    a. The Oak Ridge Boys
    b. Alabama
    c. Old Dominion
    d. Brothers Osborne

198. Dear Hate
    a. Maren Morris & Vince Gill
    b. Lady Antebellum
    c. Ashley McBryde
    d. Miranda Lambert

199. Middle of a Memory
    a. Chase Rice
    b. Chris Young
    c. Craig Morgan
    d. Cole Swindell

200. Amazed
    a. Brad Paisley
    b. Lonestar
    c. Eli Young Band
    d. Jimmie Allen

201. Heart Ache on the Dance Floor
     a. Jon Pardi
     b. John Cougar
     c. Joe Walsh
     d. Jason Aldean

202. Shameless
     a. Keith Anderson
     b. Blake Shelton
     c. Montgomery Gentry
     d. Garth Brooks

203. Ring on Every Finger
     a. Brett Young
     b. LoCash
     c. Dylan Scott
     d. Chris Young

204. Hurricane
     a. Aaron Watson
     b. Luke Combs
     c. Midland
     d. Gary Allan

205. Three Chords & The Truth
     a. Chase Rice
     b. Clint Black
     c. Clay Walker
     d. Chris Stapleton

206. Road Less Traveled
    a. Lady Antebellum
    b. Miranda Lambert
    c. Lauren Alaina
    d. Tanya Tucker

207. Last Time for Everything
    a. Dierks Bentley
    b. Brad Paisley
    c. Keith Urban
    d. Luke Bryan

208. Do I Make You Wanna
    a. Billy Currington
    b. Brett Eldredge
    c. Big & Rich
    d. Brett Young

209. Any Ol' Barstool
    a. Jake Owen
    b. Jason Aldean
    c. Justin Moore
    d. John Anderson

210. What the Hell Did I Say
    a. Kane Brown
    b. Cole Swindell
    c. Dierks Bentley
    d. Chris Stapleton

211. Hometown Girl
     a. Josh Turner
     b. Joe Diffie
     c. Clay Walker
     d. Rascal Flatts

212. Heaven
     a. Kane Brown
     b. Randy Travis
     c. Tracy Boyd
     d. Lee Brice

213. Five More Minutes
     a. Aaron Tippin
     b. Billy Dean
     c. Trace Adkins
     d. Scotty McCreery

214. Legends
     a. Kelsea Ballerini
     b. Carrie Underwood
     c. Taylor Swift
     d. Tanya Tucker

215. How Not To
     a. Ricky Van Shelton
     b. Dan & Shay
     c. Blake Shelton
     d. Granger Smith

216. Bar at the End of the World
     a. Kenny Chesney
     b. Kane Brown
     c. Keith Anderson
     d. Keith Urban

217. It Ain't My Fault
     a. Rodney Atkins
     b. Josh Turner
     c. Brothers Osborne
     d. Aaron Tippin

218. Like I Loved You
     a. Big & Rich
     b. Brett Young
     c. Brett Eldredge
     d. Brad Paisley

219. This Woman Needs
     a. SHeDAISY
     b. Kacey Musgraves
     c. Lady Antebellum
     d. Maren Morris

220. Die of a Broken Heart
     a. Carrie Underwood
     b. Kathy Mattea
     c. Shania Twain
     d. Carolyn Dawn Johnson

221. If Your Heart Ain't Busy Tonight
     a. Tanya Tucker
     b. Faith Hill
     c. Martina McBride
     d. Maren Morris

222. He Loved Me All The Way
     a. Wynonna Judd
     b. Jo Dee Messina
     c. Reba McEntire
     d. Tammy Wynette

223. Love Me Like You Used To
     a. Kelsea Ballerini
     b. Taylor Swift
     c. Tanya Tucker
     d. Trisha Yearwood

224. What if We Fly
     a. Emma Mae Jacob
     b. Jana Kramer
     c. Donna Fargo
     d. Kathy Mattea

225. If Heartaches Had Wings
     a. Shania Twain
     b. Rhonda Vincent
     c. Tanya Tucker
     d. Brenda Lee

226. XXX's and OOO's (An
     American Girl)
     a. Tanya Tucker
     b. Tammy Wynette
     c. Tori Amos
     d. Trisha Yearwood

227. He Thinks He'll Keep Her
     a. Kacey Musgraves
     b. Taylor Swift
     c. Mary Chapin Carpenter
     d. Lady Antebellum

228. Red
     a. Kathy Mattea
     b. Jo Dee Messina
     c. Taylor Swift
     d. Shania Twain

229. That Girl
     a. Jana Kramer
     b. Kate Bush
     c. Jennifer Nettles
     d. Reba McEntire

230. Shut Up and Fish
     a. Maddie & Tae
     b. Maren Morris
     c. Kathy Mattea
     d. Martina McBride

231. Love's Got an Attitude (It Is What It Is)
    a. Ashley McBryde
    b. Dixie Chicks
    c. Taylor Swift
    d. Amy Dalley

232. Someone Else's Dream
    a. Reba McEntire
    b. Faith Hill
    c. Deana Carter
    d. Carrie Underwood

233. Country Girls
    a. Deidra Whatley
    b. Kacey Musgraves
    c. Kelsea Ballerini
    d. Little Big Time

234. Just to Hear You Say That You Love Me
    a. Tammy Wynette
    b. Faith Hill & Tim McGraw
    c. Maren Morris
    d. Deana Carter

235. You Make It Easy
    a. Eagles
    b. Keith Anderson
    c. John Cougar
    d. Jason Aldean

236. Slow Burn
    a. Kacey Musgraves
    b. Kate Bush
    c. Kathy Mattea
    d. Kelsea Ballerini

237. Like We Never Loved At All
    a. Faith Hill
    b. Tanya Tucker
    c. Taylor Swift
    d. Carrie Underwood

238. Letter to Me
    a. Dierks Bentley
    b. Justin Moore
    c. Rhett Adkins
    d. Brad Paisley

239. She Don't Love You
    a. Clint Black
    b. Dave Dudley
    c. Eric Paslay
    d. Keith Whitney

240. Mama's Broken Heart
    a. Jo Dee Messina
    b. Emmylou Harris
    c. Lorrie Morgan
    d. Miranda Lambert

241. Back When
     a. Aaron Tippin
     b. Keith Whitney
     c. Tim McGraw
     d. Dierks Bentley

242. I Can Tell by The Way You Dance
     a. Keith Urban
     b. Vern Gosdin
     c. Kane Brown
     d. Keith Anderson

243. Me and My Gang
     a. Rascal Flatts
     b. Joe Walsh
     c. The Eagles
     d. Midland

244. Crazy Girl
     a. Eli Young Band
     b. Lee Brice
     c. Big & Rich
     d. Luke Bryan

245. Anything Like Me
     a. Brad Paisley
     b. Brett Eldredge
     c. Big & Rich
     d. Brooks & Dunn

246. As Good as I Once Was
    a. Travis Tritt
    b. Tim McGraw
    c. Thomas Rhett
    d. Toby Keith

247. It Just Comes Natural
    a. George Strait
    b. Gary Allan
    c. George Ducas
    d. Granger Smith

248. Greatest Love Story
    a. Jason Aldean
    b. Keith Anderson
    c. Luke Bryan
    d. LANCO

249. Just to See You Smile
    a. Tracy Boyd
    b. Tim McGraw
    c. Toby Keith
    d. Trace Adkins

250. Two Black Cadillacs
    a. Taylor Swift
    b. Carrie Underwood
    c. Lady Antebellum
    d. Kacey Musgraves

251. Bad Day of Fishin'
 a. Bryan White
 b. Billy Currington
 c. Brett Eldredge
 d. Brett Young

252. Gunpowder & Lead
 a. Tanya Tucker
 b. Jo Dee Messina
 c. Miranda Lambert
 d. Shania Twain

253. Body Like a Back Road
 a. Randy Houser
 b. Eric Church
 c. Billy Currington
 d. Sam Hunt

254. Fly Over States
 a. Jason Aldean
 b. Brett Young
 c. Chris Janson
 d. Dylan Scott

255. Kill a Word
 a. Chris Young
 b. Brett Young
 c. Eric Church & Rhiannon Giddens
 d. Luke Combs

256. Who Are You When I'm Not
     Looking
     a. Rhiannon Giddens
     b. Chase Rice
     c. Aaron Watson
     d. Midland

257. My Old Man
     a. Zac Brown Band
     b. Ryan Bingham
     c. Craig Morgan
     d. Josh Turner

258. I Got a Car
     a. Garth Brooks
     b. George Strait
     c. Guy Clark
     d. Gary Allan

259. $1000 Wedding
     a. Jamey Johnson
     b. Chris Stapleton
     c. Gram Parsons
     d. Jerry Reed

260. Stranger in My Arms
     a. Aaron Tippin
     b. Trace Adkins
     c. Merle Haggard
     d. Kris Kristofferson

261. Holding Things Together
    a. Rodney Atkins
    b. Merle Haggard
    c. Dierks Bentley
    d. Emerson Drive

262. Trying to Love Two Women
    a. Keith Urban
    b. Justin Moore
    c. The Band Perry
    d. The Oak Ridge Boys

263. Yours
    a. Jake Owen
    b. Lee Brice
    c. Brett Eldredge
    d. Russell Dickerson

264. Midnight Sun
    a. Frankie Ballard
    b. Big & Rich
    c. Garth Brooks
    d. Canaan Smith

265. I Saw God Today
    a. Luke Bryan
    b. John Cougar
    c. Joe Walsh
    d. George Strait

266. The Right Left Hand
    a. Jason Aldean
    b. George Jones
    c. Montgomery Gentry
    d. Keith Anderson

267. Papa Loved Mama
    a. Garth Brooks
    b. Florida Georgia Line
    c. The Eagles
    d. Brooks & Dunn

268. Ooh Las Vegas
    a. Alan Jackson
    b. Gram Parsons
    c. John Michael Montgomery
    d. Gary Allan

269. Home
    a. Kenny Chesney
    b. Toby Keith
    c. Clint Black
    d. Dierks Bentley

270. Same Ole Me
    a. George Jones
    b. Clay Walker
    c. Travis Tritt
    d. Brad Paisley

271. Wink
  a. Randy Travis
  b. Neal McCoy
  c. Alabama
  d. Tracy Boyd

272. Hello Mary Lou
  a. Collin Raye
  b. Statler Brothers
  c. Sawyer Brown
  d. Bryan White

273. A Man Don't Have to Die
  a. Dwight Yoakam
  b. Brad Paisley
  c. Clay Walker
  d. Vince Gill

274. Courtesy of the Red, White & Blue
   (The Angry American)
  a. Joe Diffie
  b. Toby Keith
  c. Alan Jackson
  d. Brooks & Dunn

275. Either Way
  a. Chris Stapleton
  b. Alabama
  c. Tim McGraw
  d. Rascal Flatts

276. More Than a Memory
    a. Michael Ray
    b. Old Dominion
    c. Garth Brooks
    d. Dustin Lynch

277. Rich
    a. Little Big Town
    b. Martina McBride
    c. Taylor Swift
    d. Maren Morris

278. Hangin' On
    a. Chris Young
    b. Chris Stapleton
    c. Sam Hunt
    d. Thomas Rhett

279. Drunk Me
    a. Cole Swindell
    b. Mitchell Tenpenney
    c. Scott McCreery
    d. Kane Brown

280. Shoot Me Straight
    a. Granger Smith
    b. Brothers Osborne
    c. The Oak Ridge Boys
    d. Ricky Van Shelton

281. Lose It
     a. Keith Whitley
     b. Kane Brown
     c. George Ducas
     d. Neal McCoy

282. Last Shot
     a. Kip Moore
     b. John Anderson
     c. Rhett Adkins
     d. Trace Adkins

283. Best Shot
     a. Clint Black
     b. Billy Dean
     c. Toby Keith
     d. Jimmie Allen

284. I Hate Love Songs
     a. Jo Dee Messina
     b. Shania Twain
     c. Kelsea Ballerini
     d. Taylor Swift

285. She Got The Best of Me
     a. Kenny Chesney
     b. Aaron Tippin
     c. Luke Combs
     d. Randy Travis

286. Burn Out
    a. George Strait
    b. Tim McGraw
    c. Midland
    d. Brooks & Dunn

287. Millionaire
    a. Kacey Musgraves
    b. Kelsea Ballerini
    c. Lady Antebellum
    d. Miranda Lambert

288. Life Changes
    a. Thomas Rhett
    b. Midland
    c. Aaron Watson
    d. Chase Rice

289. Sunrise, Sunburn, Sunset
    a. Luke Combs
    b. Brett Young
    c. Dylan Scott
    d. Luke Bryan

290. Simple
    a. Florida Georgia Line
    b. Chris Young
    c. Chris Janson
    d. Brett Young

291. Hotel Key
    a. Midland
    b. Brooks & Dunn
    c. Kenny Chesney
    d. Old Dominion

292. Hooked
    a. Toby Keith
    b. Clint Black
    c. Dylan Scott
    d. Rhett Adkins

293. Heart Break
    a. Lady Antebellum
    b. Kathy Mattea
    c. Faith Hill
    d. Deana Carter

294. Drunk Girl
    a. Chris Janson
    b. Dierks Bentley
    c. Keith Urban
    d. Justin Moore

295. Blue Tacoma
    a. Jake Owen
    b. Russell Dickerson
    c. Big & Rich
    d. Luke Bryan

296. Kinda Don't Care
    a. John Cougar
    b. Justin Moore
    c. Joe Walsh
    d. Jamey Johnson

297. All Day Long
    a. Garth Brooks
    b. Billy Currington
    c. Eric Church
    d. Randy Houser

298. Hide the Wine
    a. Carrie Underwood
    b. Jo Dee Messina
    c. Carly Pearce
    d. Lorrie Morgan

299. Born to Love You
    a. Rascal Flatts
    b. Keith Whitley
    c. Neal McCoy
    d. LANco

300. The Difference
    a. Billy Dean
    b. Tyler Rich
    c. Aaron Tippin
    d. Kane Brown

301. Give It Away
    a. Tim McGraw
    b. George Strait
    c. Brooks & Dunn
    d. Alan Jackson

302. When You Say Nothing At All
    a. Taylor Swift
    b. April Kry
    c. Carrie Underwood
    d. Alison Krauss

303. Magnolia Wind
    a. Faith Hill
    b. Emmylou Harris & John Prine
    c. Trisha Yearwood
    d. Little Big Town

304. I'd Have to Be Crazy
    a. Willie Nelson
    b. Johnny Cash
    c. Kenny Rogers
    d. Vince Gill

305. Grow Old with Me
    a. Gary Allan
    b. Sunny Sweeney
    c. Kenny Chesney
    d. Clint Black

306. Irma Jackson
     a. Merle Haggard
     b. Clay Walker
     c. Travis Twitt
     d. Jake Owen

307. More of You
     a. Eric Church
     b. Billy Currington
     c. Chris Stapleton
     d. Randy Houser

308. All My Exes Live in Texas
     a. Toby Keith
     b. George Strait
     c. Tim McGraw
     d. Kenny Chesney

309. In Spite of Ourselves
     a. The Eagles
     b. Florida Georgia Line
     c. John Prine & Iris DeMent
     d. Keith Anderson

310. Write This Down
     a. Montgomery Gentry
     b. Jason Aldean
     c. George Strait
     d. Joe Walsh

311. The Promise
     a. John Cougar
     b. Sturgill Simpson
     c. Dierks Bentley
     d. Justin Moore

312. Workin' For a Livin'
     a. Emerson Drive
     b. Garth Brooks
     c. Jake Owen
     d. Big & Rich

313. When You Come Back to Me Again
     a. Garth Brooks
     b. Brett Eldredge
     c. Canaan Smith
     d. Luke Bryan

314. If I Need You
     a. Brett Young
     b. Townes Van Zandt
     c. Chris Janson
     d. Dylan Scott

315. Famous
     a. Lady Antebellum
     b. Reba McEntire
     c. Tammy Wynette
     d. Deana Carter

316. 316.The Beaches of Cheyenne
    a. Chris Young
    b. Garth Brooks
    c. Chase Rice
    d. Midland

317. Standing Outside the Fire
    a. Aaron Watson
    b. Garth Brooks
    c. Luke Combs
    d. Collin Raye

318. Rodeo
    a. Garth Brooks
    b. Sawyer Brown
    c. Bryan White
    d. Clay Walker

319. My First Taste of Texas
    a. Brooks & Dunn
    b. Vince Gill
    c. Joe Diffie
    d. Ed Bruce

320. Good Ride Cowboy
    a. Alan Jackson
    b. Brooks & Dunn
    c. Tim McGraw
    d. Garth Brooks

321. Tulane Dust
     a. Rascal Flatts
     b. Merle Haggard
     c. Kenny Rogers
     d. Old Dominion

322. Southern Voice
     a. Dustin Lynch
     b. Chris Stapleton
     c. Sam Hunt
     d. Tim McGraw

323. Before He Cheats
     a. Taylor Swift
     b. Carrie Underwood
     c. Faith Hill
     d. Lorrie Morgan

324. Man! I Feel Like a Woman
     a. Shania Twain
     b. Tanya Tucker
     c. Jo Dee Messina
     d. Taylor Swift

325. American Honky Tonk Bar
     Association
     a. Don Gibson
     b. George Jones
     c. Ed Bruce
     d. Garth Brooks

326. I Always Get Lucky with You
     a. Rascal Flatts
     b. Clay Walker
     c. Collin Raye
     d. Merle Haggard

327. Always Was
     a. The Bellamy Brothers
     b. Aaron Tippin
     c. Brothers Osborne
     d. RaeLynn

328. Chattahoochee
     a. Brooks & Dunn
     b. Alan Jackson
     c. Keith Whitley
     d. Lonestar

329. Blown Away
     a. Martina McBride
     b. Carrie Underwood
     c. Trisha Yearwood
     d. Deana Carter

330. Abilene
     a. Lee Brice
     b. Waylon Jennings
     c. Big & Rich
     d. Frankie Ballard

331. Love Without End, Amen
    a. Sam Hunt
    b. Dustin Lynch
    c. Neal McCoy
    d. George Strait

332. Country Nation
    a. The Tractors
    b. Jake Owen
    c. Billy Currington
    d. Brad Paisley

333. In My Hour of Darkness
    a. Gram Parsons
    b. Dierks Bentley
    c. Luke Bryan
    d. Justin Moore

334. Does Fort Worth Ever Cross Your Mind?
    a. Kenny Chesney
    b. George Strait
    c. Little Texas
    d. Jake Owen

335. Til I Loved You
    a. Alan Jackson
    b. Big & Rich
    c. Randy Travis
    d. Restless Heart

336. Chaser
    a. Carrie Underwood
    b. Dolly Parton
    c. Trisha Yearwood
    d. Taylor Swift

337. Gone Crazy
    a. Vince Gill
    b. Merle Haggard
    c. Sam Hunt
    d. Thomas Rhett

338. The Fever
    a. Chris Stapleton
    b. Josh Turner
    c. Garth Brooks
    d. Aaron Tippin

339. Ride Me Down Easy
    a. Montgomery Gentry
    b. John Cougar
    c. Waylon Jennings
    d. Garth Brooks

340. Back When I Knew Everything
    a. Alabama
    b. The Oak Ridge Boys
    c. Aaron Tippin
    d. Aaron Watson

341. Mayberry
   a. Kris Kristofferson
   b. Rascal Flatts
   c. Brothers Osborne
   d. Aaron Watson

342. Cold Chill
   a. Keith Urban
   b. Aaron Tippin
   c. Jake Owen
   d. Sam Hunt

343. American Flag on The Moon
   a. Dustin Lynch
   b. David Allan Coe
   c. Brad Paisley
   d. Lee Brice

344. In Another's Eyes
   a. Luke Bryan
   b. Garth Brooks
   c. Clint Black
   d. Chase Rice

345. The New Soft Shoe
   a. Chris Young
   b. Craig Morgan
   c. Gram Parsons
   d. Eli Young Band

346. All In
     a. Aaron Watson
     b. Midland
     c. Luke Combs
     d. Brad Paisley

347. Baby Blue
     a. Gary Allan
     b. George Strait
     c. Old Dominion
     d. Josh Turner

348. Choctaw County Affair
     a. Lady Antebellum
     b. Dixie Chicks
     c. Ashley McBryde
     d. Carrie Underwood

349. A Song for You
     a. Eagles
     b. Gram Parsons
     c. Joe Walsh
     d. Midland

350. I Like The Sound of That
     a. Kane Brown
     b. Rascal Flatts
     c. Kenny Chesney
     d. Keith Anderson

351. Ocean Front Property
    a. Dierks Bentley
    b. George Strait
    c. Justin Moore
    d. Rhett Atkins

352. Dying To See Her
    a. Brad Paisley
    b. Aaron Tippin
    c. Keith Whitley
    d. Big & Rich

353. Little Man
    a. Luke Bryan
    b. Big & Rich
    c. Alan Jackson
    d. George Jones

354. For You I Will
    a. John Michael Montgomery
    b. Jason Aldean
    c. Aaron Tippin
    d. Keith Anderson

355. Honky Tonk Night Time Man
    a. Merle Haggard
    b. Garth Brooks
    c. Brooks & Dunn
    d. Eagles

356. Learning to Live Again
     a. Garth Brooks
     b. Alan Jackson
     c. Gary Allen
     d. Aaron Tippin

357. Church Bells
     a. Emmylou Harris
     b. Carrie Underwood
     c. Dixie Chicks
     d. Taylor Swift

358. Burning Memories
     a. Waylon Jennings
     b. Luke Bryan
     c. Big & Rich
     d. Justin Moore

359. You Don't Have Very Far to Go
     a. Merle Haggard
     b. Johnny Lee
     c. Jason Aldean
     d. Sawyer Brown

360. Love And War
     a. Old Dominion
     b. Collin Raye
     c. Dustin Lynch
     d. Brad Paisley

361. She
   a. Clay Walker
   b. Gram Parsons
   c. Ronnie Milsap
   d. Ricky Van Shelton

362. Gone Green
   a. Keith Urban
   b. Garth Brooks
   c. Canaan Smith
   d. Brad Paisley

363. Prayin' for Daylight
   a. Luke Bryan
   b. Rascal Flatts
   c. Jason Aldean
   d. Keith Anderson

364. I Cross My Heart
   a. Joe Walsh
   b. Florida Georgia Line
   c. George Strait
   d. John Cougar

365. Friends in Low Places
   a. Billy Currington
   b. Randy Houser
   c. Garth Brooks
   d. Aaron Tippin

366. Brass Buttons
    a. Big & Rich
    b. Jake Owen
    c. Keith Urban
    d. Gram Parsons

367. Here in The Real World
    a. Sam Hunt
    b. Billy Currington
    c. Neal McCoy
    d. Alan Jackson

368. Changed
    a. Dustin Lynch
    b. Keith Whitley
    c. Rascal Flatts
    d. Tim McGraw

369. Take Me There
    a. Eric Church
    b. Rascal Flatts
    c. Dierks Bentley
    d. Kenny Chesney

370. Check Yes Or No
    a. Old Dominion
    b. George Strait
    c. Dustin Lynch
    d. Clint Black

371. Ever Ever After
     a. Carrie Underwood
     b. Maren Morris
     c. Reba McEntire
     d. Little Big Town

372. Two of a Kind, Workin on a
     Full House
     a. Chris Janson
     b. Garth Brooks
     c. Cole Swindell
     d. Kane Brown

373. Her
     a. John Anderson
     b. Keith Whitley
     c. Aaron Tippin
     d. Neal McCoy

374. Time is Love
     a. Josh Turner
     b. David Allan Coe
     c. Rodney Atkins
     d. Randy Travis

375. Forever Changed
     a. Crystal Gayle
     b. Taylor Swift
     c. Carrie Underwood
     d. Tanya Tucker

376. Always Be Mine
    a. Eric Church
    b. The Oak Ridge Boys
    c. Craig Morgan
    d. John Conlee

377. Don't
    a. Rhett Atkins
    b. Billy Currington
    c. Dierks Bentley
    d. Ray Price

378. Chasin' That Neon Rainbow
    a. John Cougar
    b. Alan Jackson
    c. Morgan Wallen
    d. Gary Allan

379. Hot Burrito #1
    a. Trace Boyd
    b. Gram Parsons
    c. Kane Brown
    d. Craig Morgan

380. Linda on My Mind
    a. Vince Gill
    b. Conway Twitty
    c. Joe Diffie
    d. Alan Jackson

381. What Hurts The Most
    a. Sawyer Brown
    b. Rascal Flatts
    c. Collin Raye
    d. Bryan White

382. Me and God'll Go On Loving
    a. Kenny Chesney
    b. Toby Keith
    c. Josh Turner
    d. Craig Morgan

383. 383.Wishing All of These Old Things Were New
    a. The Oak Ridge Boys
    b. Eagles
    c. Merle Haggard
    d. Old Dominion

384. I'll Go On Loving You
    a. Aaron Watson
    b. Alabama
    c. Alan Jackson
    d. Aaron Tippin

385. Old Alabama
    a. Brad Paisley
    b. Alabama
    c. Brothers Osborne
    d. Billy Dean

386. Ain't Goin Down ('Til The Sun Comes Up)
   a. Garth Brooks
   b. Blake Shelton
   c. Keith Anderson
   d. Clint Black

387. Me and Bobby Mcgee
   a. Rascal Flatts
   b. Midland
   c. Keith Whitley
   d. Waylon Jennings

388. I'm Leaving
   a. Eli Young Band
   b. Aaron Tippin
   c. Midland
   d. Jason Aldean

389. Enjoy Yourself
   a. Thomas Rhett
   b. Brooks & Dunn
   c. Billy Currington
   d. Randy Travis

390. Longneck Bottle
   a. Luke Combs
   b. Chase Rice
   c. Garth Brooks
   d. Dylan Scott

391. Tight Fittin' Jeans
    a. Old Dominion
    b. Midland
    c. Conway Twitty
    d. Florida Georgia Line

392. Country Boys
    a. Clint Black
    b. Chris Young
    c. Chris Janson
    d. Craig Morgan

393. Dirty Laundry
    a. Kacey Musgraves
    b. Carrie Underwood
    c. Lady Antebellum
    d. Little Big Town

394. All Over Me
    a. Tracy Boyd
    b. John Legend
    c. Garth Brooks
    d. Travis Tritt

395. Blame Me
    a. George Ezra
    b. Tracy Boyd
    c. Billy Currington
    d. Brett Young

396. Hickory Wind
    a. Gram Parsons
    b. Toby Keith
    c. Trace Adkins
    d. Randy Travis

397. Perfect Storm
    a. Brad Paisley
    b. Clay Walker
    c. Dustin Lynch
    d. Eric Church

398. Every Reason Not to Go
    a. Brett Eldredge
    b. Keith Urban
    c. Billy Currington
    d. Dierks Bentley

399. Your Man
    a. Brett Young
    b. Chris Janson
    c. Dierks Bentley
    d. Josh Turner

400. Lost
    a. Midland
    b. Aaron Watson
    c. Aaron Tippin
    d. Chase Rice

401. Carrying Your Love with Me
    a. Luke Combs
    b. Brett Young
    c. George Strait
    d. Chris Young

402. To Make You Feel My Love
    a. Dylan Scott
    b. Garth Brooks
    c. Montgomery Gentry
    d. Keith Anderson

403. Roses in The Winter
    a. John Cougar
    b. Merle Haggard
    c. Justin Moore
    d. Jake Owen

404. Crazy Dreams
    a. Miranda Lambert
    b. Lady Antebellum
    c. Ashley McBryde
    d. Carrie Underwood

405. Last Name
    a. Jo Dee Messina
    b. Carrie Underwood
    c. Faith Hill
    d. Tanya Tucker

406. The Chair
  a. Kenny Chesney
  b. Trace Adkins
  c. George Strait
  d. Rodney Atkins

407. Everything
  a. Billy Currington
  b. Eric Church
  c. Luke Bryan
  d. Big & Rich

408. We Shall Be Free
  a. Little Texas
  b. Garth Brooks
  c. Justin Moore
  d. Keith Urban

409. Drive (For Daddy Gene)
  a. Alan Jackson
  b. Dustin Lynch
  c. The Oak Ridge Boys
  d. Randy Travis

410. Without a Fight
  a. Billy Currington
  b. Brad Paisley
  c. Brett Eldredge
  d. Brett Young

411. Oh Love
    a. Carrie Underwood
    b. Miranda Lambert
    c. Lady Antebellum
    d. Taylor Swift

412. Ain't Your Memory Got No Pride
    at All
    a. Michael Ray
    b. Midland
    c. Merle Haggard
    d. Montgomery Gentry

413. Bless the Broken Road
    a. Randy Travis
    b. Ryan Bingham
    c. Rascal Flatts
    d. Randy Houser

414. Landslide
    a. Deana Carter
    b. Maren Morris
    c. LeAnn Rimes
    d. Taylor Swift

415. Would You Go with Me
    a. Joe Diffie
    b. John Anderson
    c. Josh Turner
    d. John Michael Montgomery

416. Mona Lisa
     a. Conway Twitty
     b. Clay Walker
     c. Clint Black
     d. Craig Morgan

417. The Dance
     a. Brett Young
     b. Chris Janson
     c. Dylan Scott
     d. Garth Brooks

418. Love Me Back
     a. Chris Young
     b. Aaron Tippin
     c. Brett Young
     d. Luke Combs

419. Good Night
     a. Chase Rice
     b. Aaron Watson
     c. Midland
     d. Billy Currington

420. Return of The Grievous Angel
     a. Craig Morgan
     b. Josh Turner
     c. Gram Parsons
     d. Guy Clark

421. Gone Country
     a. Jamey Johnson
     b. Chris Stapleton
     c. Alan Jackson
     d. Jerry Reed

422. Why Don't We Just Dance
     a. Aaron Tippin
     b. Josh Turner
     c. Trace Adkins
     d. Kris Kristofferson

423. It Don't Hurt Like It Used To
     a. Joe Walsh
     b. Billy Currington
     c. Eric Church
     d. Randy Houser

424. Cowboy and Clown
     a. George Strait
     b. Craig Morgan
     c. Tim McGraw
     d. Brooks & Dunn

425. These Days
     a. Rascal Flatts
     b. Alan Jackson
     c. John Michael Montgomery
     d. Gary Allen

426. If Only I Could Fly
    a. Kenny Chesney
    b. Merle Haggard
    c. Toby Keith
    d. Clint Black

427. Long Black Train
    a. Josh Turner
    b. Clay Walker
    c. Travis Tritt
    d. Brad Paisley

428. The Thunder Rolls
    a. Alabama
    b. Garth Brooks
    c. Tracy Boyd
    d. Randy Travis

429. Slow Hand
    a. Dierks Bentley
    b. Conway Twitty
    c. Emerson Drive
    d. The Tractors

430. Everywhere I Go
    a. Craig Morgan
    b. Keith Urban
    c. Justin Moore
    d. Trace Adkins

431. I'm Movin' On
    a. Jake Owen
    b. Lee Brice
    c. Rascal Flatts
    d. Brett Eldredge

432. Bad Man
    a. Keith Whitley
    b. Josh Turner
    c. Collin Raye
    d. Conway Twitty

433. Good Girl
    a. Deana Carter
    b. Carrie Underwood
    c. Martina McBride
    d. Trisha Yearwood

434. Firecracker
    a. Big & Rich
    b. Josh Turner
    c. Lee Brice
    d. Sam Hunt

435. A Simple Country Girl
    a. Jake Owen
    b. Conway Twitty
    c. Dustin Lynch
    d. Neal McCoy

436. Love Done Gone
 a. Brad Paisley
 b. Billy Currington
 c. Little Big Town
 d. Dixie Chicks

437. Everything is Fine
 a. Josh Turner
 b. Luke Combs
 c. Luke Bryan
 d. Neal McCoy

438. Next in Line
 a. Sawyer Brown
 b. Collin Raye
 c. Conway Twitty
 d. Bryan White

439. Unanswered Prayers
 a. Clay Walker
 b. Vince Gill
 c. Joe Diffie
 d. Garth Brooks

440. I See the Want in Your Eyes
 a. Alabama
 b. Conway Twitty
 c. Alan Jackson
 d. Brooks & Dunn

441. Just Stand Up
    a. Dixie Chicks
    b. Little Big Town
    c. Carrie Underwood
    d. Kate Bush

442. Fish Weren't Bitin'
    a. Tim McGraw
    b. Craig Morgan
    c. Rascal Flatts
    d. Johnny Cash

443. A Man Alone
    a. Conway Twitty
    b. Kenny Rogers
    c. Michael Ray
    d. Old Dominion

444. It Took a Woman
    a. Craig Morgan
    b. Dustin Lynch
    c. Chris Stapleton
    d. Sam Hunt

445. Swingin'
    a. Thomas Rhett
    b. Cole Swindell
    c. Scott McCreery
    d. John Anderson

446. Goodbye Earl
    a. Grace Jones
    b. Dixie Chicks
    c. Tina Turner
    d. Martina McBride

447. The Kiss
    a. Faith Hill
    b. Loretta Lynn
    c. Taylor Swift
    d. Kelsea Ballerini

448. Should've Been a Cowboy
    a. Kane Brown
    b. Granger Smith
    c. Brothers Osborne
    d. Toby Keith

449. Straight Tequila Night
    a. The Oak Ridge Boys
    b. Ricky Van Shelton
    c. John Anderson
    d. Keith Whitley

450. I just can't Live A Lie
    a. April Kry
    b. Carrie Underwood
    c. Jana Kramer
    d. Maren Morris

451. Beer Run
    a. George Ducas
    b. Neal McCoy
    c. Garth Brooks
    d. John Anderson

452. Fancy
    a. Deana Carter
    b. Reba McEntire
    c. Tammy Wynette
    d. Faith Hill

453. Fancy Free
    a. Rhett Adkins
    b. The Oakridge Boys
    c. Trace Adkins
    d. Clint Black

454. Need You Now
    a. Lady Antebellum
    b. Reba McEntire
    c. Dolly Parton
    d. Kathy Mattea

455. Strawberry Wine
    a. Trisha Yearwood
    b. Patty Loveless
    c. Lorrie Morgan
    d. Deana Carter

456. Where Were You (When the World
     Stopped Turning)
     a. Billy Dean
     b. Alan Jackson
     c. Toby Keith
     d. Aaron Tippin

457. Somebody Lied
     a. Kenny Chesney
     b. Randy Travis
     c. Ricky Van Shelton
     d. Dierks Bentley

458. Talladega
     a. Eagles
     b. Eric Church
     c. Aaron Watson
     d. Midland

459. Stand by Your Man
     a. Shania Twain
     b. Jo Dee Messina
     c. Tammy Wynette
     d. Tanya Tucker

460. Take Me Home Country Roads
     a. The Oak Ridge Boys
     b. Florida Georgia Line
     c. John Denver
     d. Willie Nelson

461. 461.Chicken Fried
    a. The Tractors
    b. Zac Brown Band
    c. Emerson Drive
    d. Keith Urban

462. Cowboy Take Me Away
    a. Kacey Musgraves
    b. Dixie Chicks
    c. Miranda Lambert
    d. Ashley McBryde

463. 463.Eighteen Wheels and a
    Dozen Roses
    a. Lady Antebellum
    b. Kelsea Ballerini
    c. Kathy Mattea
    d. Taylor Swift

464. I May Hate Myself in the Morning
    a. Loretta Lynn
    b. Lee Ann Womack
    c. Carrie Underwood
    d. Dolly Parton

465. Baby Girl
    a. Lorrie Morgan
    b. Tanya Tucker
    c. Sugarland
    d. Jo Dee Messina

466. I fall to Pieces
    a. Nina Simone
    b. Pam Tillis
    c. Tori Amos
    d. Patsy Cline

467. Your Cheatin' Heart
    a. Hank Williams
    b. Randy Houser
    c. Eric Church
    d. Billy Currington

468. D-I-V-O-R-C-E
    a. Maren Morris
    b. Deana Carter
    c. Tammy Wynette
    d. Faith Hill

469. The River
    a. Joe Walsh
    b. Ryan Bingham
    c. Craig Morgan
    d. Garth Brooks

470. Drop On By
    a. April Kry
    b. Jana Kramer
    c. Taylor Swift
    d. Laura Bell Bundy

471. I Hope You Dance
    a. Jo Dee Messina
    b. Lee Ann Womack
    c. Shania Twain
    d. Trisha Yearwood

472. Ladies Love Country Boys
    a. Josh Turner
    b. Trace Adkins
    c. Guy Clark
    d. Jamey Johnson

473. Don't Let Me Be Lonely
    a. Alabama
    b. The Band Perry
    c. Florida Georgia Line
    d. Little Big Town

474. Leave a Light On
    a. Garth Brooks
    b. Chris Stapleton
    c. Jerry Reed
    d. Aaron Tippin

475. I'll Think of a Reason Later
    a. Jo Dee Messina
    b. Tanya Tucker
    c. Lee Ann Womack
    d. Taylor Swift

476. That Summer
     a. Thomas Adkins
     b. Garth Brooks
     c. Kris Kristofferson
     d. Rodney Atkins

477. That's How Country Boys Roll
     a. George Strait
     b. Tim McGraw
     c. Brooks & Dunn
     d. Billy Currington

478. Angels Fall Sometimes
     a. Alan Jackson
     b. John Michael Montgomery
     c. Gary Allan
     d. Josh Turner

479. A Little Past a Rock
     a. Lee Ann Womack
     b. Kelsea Ballerini
     c. Lady Antebellum
     d. Ashley McBryde

480. Callin' Baton Rouge
     a. Kenny Chesney
     b. Toby Keith
     c. Garth Brooks
     d. Clint Black

481. I'm Beginning to See The Light
    a. Clay Walker
    b. Garth Brooks
    c. Travis Tritt
    d. Brad Paisley

482. Chrome
    a. Randy Travis
    b. Trace Adkins
    c. Tracy Boyd
    d. Alabama

483. A Song for Ruby
    a. Dierks Bentley
    b. Conway Twitty
    c. Emerson Drive
    d. Keith Urban

484. Does My Ring Burn Your Finger
    a. Tina Turner
    b. Martina McBride
    c. Lee Ann Womack
    d. Deana Carter

485. A Little of You
    a. Conway Twitty
    b. Justin Moore
    c. The Band Perry
    d. Jake Owen

486. Wrapped Up in You
   a. Garth Brooks
   b. Lee Brice
   c. Brett Eldredge
   d. Frankie Ballard

487. I Want Us Back
   a. Big & Rich
   b. Canaan Smith
   c. Craig Morgan
   d. Luke Bryan

488. Bottom of the Barrel
   a. Maren Morris
   b. April Kry
   c. Reba McEntire
   d. Lee Ann Womack

489. Arlington
   a. Luke Bryan
   b. Brett Young
   c. Chris Janson
   d. Trace Adkins

490. He'll Be Back
   a. Loretta Lynn
   b. Lee Ann Womack
   c. Little Big Town
   d. Lorrie Morgan

491. Wake Me Up
      a. Billy Currington
      b. Luke Combs
      c. Chase Rice
      d. Aaron Watson

492. Two Pina Coladas
      a. Garth Brooks
      b. Chris Young
      c. John Cougar
      d. Joe Walsh

493. Songs about Me
      a. Clint Black
      b. Trace Adkins
      c. Dierks Bentley
      d. Big & Rich

494. Cowboys Forever
      a. Trace Adkins
      b. Garth Brooks
      c. Clay Walker
      d. Justin Moore

495. Every Light in The House is On
      a. Rascal Flatts
      b. Blake Shelton
      c. Josh Turner
      d. Trace Adkins

496. My Kind of Woman
    a. Brett Eldredge
    b. Montgomery Gentry
    c. Toby Keith
    d. Craig Morgan

497. I'd Love to Lay You Down
    a. Eric Church
    b. Conway Twitty
    c. Alan Jackson
    d. Brooks & Dunn

498. If These Walls Could Talk
    a. Trisha Yearwood
    b. Deana Carter
    c. Lee Ann Womack
    d. Emmylou Harris

499. A Mighty Good God
    a. Luke Bryan
    b. Trace Adkins
    c. Eagles
    d. John Cougar

500. What's She Doing Now
    a. Alan Jackson
    b. Brooks & Dunn
    c. Garth Brooks & George Strait
    d. The Oak Ridge Boys

Answers - Country Music

1. B	38. B	75. D	112. C	149. C	186. C	223. C
2. D	39. A	76. B	113. C	150. A	187. C	224. A
3. B	40. C	77. B	114. B	151. B	188. C	225. B
4. D	41. B	78. A	115. A	152. B	189. D	226. D
5. C	42. A	79. C	116. D	153. C	190. A	227. C
6. B	43. C	80. D	117. B	154. A	191. B	228. C
7. A	44. C	81. C	118. C	155. B	192. A	229. C
8. D	45. D	82. A	119. B	156. D	193. A	230. A
9. A	46. A	83. D	120. D	157. A	194. C	231. D
10. C	47. C	84. A	121. D	158. C	195. B	232. B
11. B	48. A	85. A	122. A	159. A	196. D	233. A
12. C	49. D	86. C	123. C	160. B	197. C	234. B
13. C	50. A	87. A	124. B	161. B	198. A	235. D
14. A	51. B	88. A	125. A	162. B	199. D	236. A
15. D	52. C	89. C	126. C	163. C	200. B	237. A
16. B	53. A	90. A	127. A	164. D	201. A	238. D
17. A	54. B	91. A	128. B	165. C	202. D	239. C
18. B	55. D	92. B	129. B	166. A	203. B	240. D
19. D	56. A	93. B	130. A	167. C	204. B	241. C
20. B	57. A	94. A	131. C	168. B	205. A	242. B
21. C	58. A	95. D	132. A	169. A	206. C	243. A
22. A	59. C	96. C	133. A	170. D	207. B	244. A
23. A	60. C	97. B	134. A	171. C	208. A	245. A
24. B	61. D	98. A	135. C	172. B	209. B	246. D
25. D	62. C	99. D	136. B	173. D	210. C	247. A
26. C	63. B	100. B	137. D	174. A	211. A	248. D
27. A	64. A	101. C	138. A	175. B	212. A	249. B
28. B	65. D	102. D	139. D	176. D	213. D	250. B
29. A	66. A	103. A	140. B	177. A	214. A	251. B
30. B	67. B	104. C	141. B	178. B	215. B	252. C
31. D	68. A	105. B	142. C	179. C	216. A	253. D
32. A	69. C	106. B	143. A	180. A	217. C	254. A
33. A	70. A	107. D	144. C	181. D	218. B	255. C
34. D	71. B	108. D	145. C	182. C	219. A	256. A
35. B	72. C	109. A	146. A	183. B	220. D	257. A
36. A	73. C	110. D	147. D	184. D	221. A	258. B
37. C	74. A	111. B	148. A	185. A	222. D	259. C

Answers - Country Music

260. C	297. A	334. B	371. A	408. B	445. D	482. B
261. B	298. C	335. A	372. B	409. A	446. B	483. B
262. D	299. D	336. A	373. C	410. B	447. A	484. C
263. D	300. B	337. B	374. A	411. A	448. D	485. A
264. C	301. B	338. C	375. C	412. C	449. C	486. A
265. D	302. D	339. C	376. C	413. C	450. B	487. C
266. B	303. B	340. C	377. B	414. C	451. C	488. D
267. A	304. A	341. B	378. B	415. C	452. B	489. D
268. B	305. B	342. B	379. B	416. A	453. B	490. B
269. D	306. A	343. C	380. B	417. D	454. A	491. A
270. A	307. C	344. B	381. B	418. B	455. D	492. A
271. B	308. B	345. C	382. C	419. D	456. B	493. B
272. B	309. C	346. D	383. C	420. C	457. C	494. B
273. B	310. C	347. B	384. C	421. C	458. B	495. D
274. B	311. B	348. D	385. A	422. B	459. C	496. D
275. A	312. B	349. B	386. A	423. B	460. C	497. B
276. C	313. A	350. B	387. D	424. B	461. B	498. C
277. D	314. B	351. B	388. B	425. A	462. B	499. B
278. A	315. A	352. A	389. C	426. B	463. C	500. C
279. B	316. B	353. C	390. C	427. A	464. B	
280. B	317. B	354. C	391. C	428. B	465. C	
281. B	318. A	355. A	392. D	429. B	466. D	
282. A	319. A	356. A	393. B	430. A	467. A	
283. D	320. D	357. B	394. B	431. C	468. C	
284. C	321. B	358. A	395. A	432. D	469. D	
285. C	322. D	359. A	396. A	433. B	470. D	
286. C	323. B	360. D	397. A	434. B	471. B	
287. C	324. A	361. B	398. C	435. B	472. B	
288. A	325. D	362. D	399. D	436. B	473. B	
289. D	326. D	363. B	400. C	437. A	474. A	
290. A	327. B	364. C	401. C	438. C	475. C	
291. D	328. B	365. C	402. B	439. D	476. B	
292. C	329. B	366. D	403. B	440. B	477. D	
293. A	330. B	367. D	404. D	441. C	478. D	
294. A	331. D	368. C	405. B	442. B	479. A	
295. B	332. D	369. B	406. C	443. A	480. C	
296. B	333. A	370. B	407. A	444. A	481. B	

Worksheet

FOLD

1.__☐	38.__☐	75.__☐	112.__☐	149.__☐	186.__☐	223.__☐
2.__☐	39.__☐	76.__☐	113.__☐	150.__☐	187.__☐	224.__☐
3.__☐	40.__☐	77.__☐	114.__☐	151.__☐	188.__☐	225.__☐
4.__☐	41.__☐	78.__☐	115.__☐	152.__☐	189.__☐	226.__☐
5.__☐	42.__☐	79.__☐	116.__☐	153.__☐	190.__☐	227.__☐
6.__☐	43.__☐	80.__☐	117.__☐	154.__☐	191.__☐	228.__☐
7.__☐	44.__☐	81.__☐	118.__☐	155.__☐	192.__☐	229.__☐
8.__☐	45.__☐	82.__☐	119.__☐	156.__☐	193.__☐	230.__☐
9.__☐	46.__☐	83.__☐	120.__☐	157.__☐	194.__☐	231.__☐
10.__☐	47.__☐	84.__☐	121.__☐	158.__☐	195.__☐	232.__☐
11.__☐	48.__☐	85.__☐	122.__☐	159.__☐	196.__☐	233.__☐
12.__☐	49.__☐	86.__☐	123.__☐	160.__☐	197.__☐	234.__☐
13.__☐	50.__☐	87.__☐	124.__☐	161.__☐	198.__☐	235.__☐
14.__☐	51.__☐	88.__☐	125.__☐	162.__☐	199.__☐	236.__☐
15.__☐	52.__☐	89.__☐	126.__☐	163.__☐	200.__☐	237.__☐
16.__☐	53.__☐	90.__☐	127.__☐	164.__☐	201.__☐	238.__☐
17.__☐	54.__☐	91.__☐	128.__☐	165.__☐	202.__☐	239.__☐
18.__☐	55.__☐	92.__☐	129.__☐	166.__☐	203.__☐	240.__☐
19.__☐	56.__☐	93.__☐	130.__☐	167.__☐	204.__☐	241.__☐
20.__☐	57.__☐	94.__☐	131.__☐	168.__☐	205.__☐	242.__☐
21.__☐	58.__☐	95.__☐	132.__☐	169.__☐	206.__☐	243.__☐
22.__☐	59.__☐	96.__☐	133.__☐	170.__☐	207.__☐	244.__☐
23.__☐	60.__☐	97.__☐	134.__☐	171.__☐	208.__☐	245.__☐
24.__☐	61.__☐	98.__☐	135.__☐	172.__☐	209.__☐	246.__☐
25.__☐	62.__☐	99.__☐	136.__☐	173.__☐	210.__☐	247.__☐
26.__☐	63.__☐	100.__☐	137.__☐	174.__☐	211.__☐	248.__☐
27.__☐	64.__☐	101.__☐	138.__☐	175.__☐	212.__☐	249.__☐
28.__☐	65.__☐	102.__☐	139.__☐	176.__☐	213.__☐	250.__☐
29.__☐	66.__☐	103.__☐	140.__☐	177.__☐	214.__☐	251.__☐
30.__☐	67.__☐	104.__☐	141.__☐	178.__☐	215.__☐	252.__☐
31.__☐	68.__☐	105.__☐	142.__☐	179.__☐	216.__☐	253.__☐
32.__☐	69.__☐	106.__☐	143.__☐	180.__☐	217.__☐	254.__☐
33.__☐	70.__☐	107.__☐	144.__☐	181.__☐	218.__☐	255.__☐
34.__☐	71.__☐	108.__☐	145.__☐	182.__☐	219.__☐	256.__☐
35.__☐	72.__☐	109.__☐	146.__☐	183.__☐	220.__☐	257.__☐
36.__☐	73.__☐	110.__☐	147.__☐	184.__☐	221.__☐	258.__☐
37.__☐	74.__☐	111.__☐	148.__☐	185.__☐	222.__☐	259.__☐

You can copy both sides of this worksheet and use it to record your answers. Then check off the correct answers by folding alongside the column and holding next to the Answer Sheet.

Worksheet

260. ☐	297. ☐	334. ☐	371. ☐	408. ☐	445. ☐	482. ☐
261. ☐	298. ☐	335. ☐	372. ☐	409. ☐	446. ☐	483. ☐
262. ☐	299. ☐	336. ☐	373. ☐	410. ☐	447. ☐	484. ☐
263. ☐	300. ☐	337. ☐	374. ☐	411. ☐	448. ☐	485. ☐
264. ☐	301. ☐	338. ☐	375. ☐	412. ☐	449. ☐	486. ☐
265. ☐	302. ☐	339. ☐	376. ☐	413. ☐	450. ☐	487. ☐
266. ☐	303. ☐	340. ☐	377. ☐	414. ☐	451. ☐	488. ☐
267. ☐	304. ☐	341. ☐	378. ☐	415. ☐	452. ☐	489. ☐
268. ☐	305. ☐	342. ☐	379. ☐	416. ☐	453. ☐	490. ☐
269. ☐	306. ☐	343. ☐	380. ☐	417. ☐	454. ☐	491. ☐
270. ☐	307. ☐	344. ☐	381. ☐	418. ☐	455. ☐	492. ☐
271. ☐	308. ☐	345. ☐	382. ☐	419. ☐	456. ☐	493. ☐
272. ☐	309. ☐	346. ☐	383. ☐	420. ☐	457. ☐	494. ☐
273. ☐	310. ☐	347. ☐	384. ☐	421. ☐	458. ☐	495. ☐
274. ☐	311. ☐	348. ☐	385. ☐	422. ☐	459. ☐	496. ☐
275. ☐	312. ☐	349. ☐	386. ☐	423. ☐	460. ☐	497. ☐
276. ☐	313. ☐	350. ☐	387. ☐	424. ☐	461. ☐	498. ☐
277. ☐	314. ☐	351. ☐	388. ☐	425. ☐	462. ☐	499. ☐
278. ☐	315. ☐	352. ☐	389. ☐	426. ☐	463. ☐	500. ☐
279. ☐	316. ☐	353. ☐	390. ☐	427. ☐	464. ☐	
280. ☐	317. ☐	354. ☐	391. ☐	428. ☐	465. ☐	
281. ☐	318. ☐	355. ☐	392. ☐	429. ☐	466. ☐	
282. ☐	319. ☐	356. ☐	393. ☐	430. ☐	467. ☐	
283. ☐	320. ☐	357. ☐	394. ☐	431. ☐	468. ☐	
284. ☐	321. ☐	358. ☐	395. ☐	432. ☐	469. ☐	
285. ☐	322. ☐	359. ☐	396. ☐	433. ☐	470. ☐	
286. ☐	323. ☐	360. ☐	397. ☐	434. ☐	471. ☐	
287. ☐	324. ☐	361. ☐	398. ☐	435. ☐	472. ☐	
288. ☐	325. ☐	362. ☐	399. ☐	436. ☐	473. ☐	
289. ☐	326. ☐	363. ☐	400. ☐	437. ☐	474. ☐	
290. ☐	327. ☐	364. ☐	401. ☐	438. ☐	475. ☐	
291. ☐	328. ☐	365. ☐	402. ☐	439. ☐	476. ☐	
292. ☐	329. ☐	366. ☐	403. ☐	440. ☐	477. ☐	
293. ☐	330. ☐	367. ☐	404. ☐	441. ☐	478. ☐	
294. ☐	331. ☐	368. ☐	405. ☐	442. ☐	479. ☐	
295. ☐	332. ☐	369. ☐	406. ☐	443. ☐	480. ☐	
296. ☐	333. ☐	370. ☐	407. ☐	444. ☐	481. ☐	

CPSIA information can be obtained
at www.ICGtesting.com
Printed in the USA
BVHW031539121122
651573BV00008B/661